D1800778

```
37653014714649
Main NonFiction: 1st flr
811 SQUIRES
Gardens of the world :
poems
```

AUG 81

CENTRAL ARKANSAS LIBRARY SYSTEM
LITTLE ROCK PUBLIC LIBRARY
700 LOUISIANA
LITTLE ROCK, ARKANSAS

Gardens of the World

Other Books by the Same Author

POETRY
Cornar
Where the Compass Spins
Fingers of Hermes
The Light Under Islands
Daedalus
Waiting in the Bone
Journeys

PROSE
The Loyalties of Robinson Jeffers
The Major Themes of Robert Frost
Frederic Prokosch
Allen Tate: A Literary Biography
[Editor] Allen Tate and His Work: Critical Evaluations

Gardens of the World

*Poems by
Radcliffe Squires*

Louisiana State University Press
BATON ROUGE AND LONDON   1981

Copyright © 1981 by Radcliffe Squires
All rights reserved
Manufactured in the United States of America

Designer: Joanna Hill
Typeface: Janson
Typesetter: Service Typesetters
Printer and Binder: Thomson-Shore, Inc.

A number of these poems first appeared in the following publications: *Changes, Chicago Tribune Sunday Magazine, Counter/Measures, Empyrea, Hudson Review, Michigan Quarterly Review, Nation, Southern Review, Shenandoah, Vanderbilt Poetry Review,* and *World Order.*

"The Garden of Medusa," "The Garden of Hecate," "The Garden of Ariadne," "The Garden of Maia," and "The Garden of the World" were published in *Sewanee Review,* LXXXIII (Summer, 1975). Copyright 1975 by Radcliffe Squires. "News from the Island Where Executioners Are Exiled" was published in *Sewanee Review,* LXXXVII (Summer, 1979). Copyright 1979 by Radcliffe Squires.

About half of these poems were previously published in a limited edition, *Waiting in the Bone,* produced by the Cummington Press and Abattoir Editions, copyright 1973 Radcliffe Squires.

LIBRARY OF CONGRESS CATALOGING IN PUBLICATION INFORMATION

Squires, James Radcliffe, 1917–
   Gardens of the world.

  I. Title.
PS3537.Q68G37 811'.52   80-21750
ISBN 0-8071-0754-9
ISBN 0-8071-0755-7 (pbk.)

For Michael Bundrage

Contents

I
A Day in Salamanca 3
Animal Crossing 5
A March on Washington 6
Christmas at the End of a Decade 8
New Year's Day at the End of a Decade 9
Waiting in the Bone 10
The Castrato Singer 13
In the Gallery 14
Ramifications 15
Old Leaves 16
Frost Line 17
The Sons of Medea 18
Men and Horses: Wyoming 20
The Water Hole 22
Vermilion Cliffs 23
Storm in the Desert 24
Falcons Hooded and Perched 26
Spring 27

II
Three Birds in Winter 31
Music of Disaster 32
News from the Island Where Executioners Are Exiled 33

The First Day out from Troy   34
The Cave of Hermes   36
Winchester   37
Lines for the English   38
Some Marvelous Quarry   39
First Day of School   40
Achilles and the Tortoise   42
Heliogabalus   43
Chasms   44

III
The Garden of Medusa   47
The Garden of Hecate   49
The Garden of Eros   51
The Garden of Aphrodite   52
The Garden of Ariadne   53
The Garden of Maia   55
The Garden of the World   57
The Garden of Niobe   58
The Garden of Prometheus   60

I

A Day in Salamanca

Across the square
The late sun angles down through arches
In golden cones against the violet
Shop windows. At a near table
A beautiful priest smiles at his expensive
Dessert; at another table, students, old-looking in
Their dark suits, talk erotically of revolution.
Then priest and students turn toward me with
The squint of conspirators
While a boy, leaning into the slanted sunlight
As though it were wind, comes slowly
Across the immense square, tacking into the light,
Until he stands at my table.
His big wrists glow six inches
Beyond the scarecrow sleeves,
As he holds a sparrow toward me
And chants: "Which shall it be, freedom
Or blood-sacrifice?"
                      The bird peers
From the noose of thumb and forefinger,
Tightening to show the way of sacrifice.
I laugh. The boy scowls, his lips
Curl back from wet teeth. He pushes nearer,
A windowless smell of cooking oil comes
From his clothes, but beneath that, faintly,
The neutral perfume of all humanity, the smell
(I think) of wheat fields motionless in sunlight.
I lean back, shrug, and say he does not have
The courage to kill a bird. The insult brings
The moment we have all waited for. The priest
Titters, the students freeze. The boy's face,
Pressing nearer, blots out the square with
Its false sunset, whispering, "*Libertad o sacrificio?*"
And I drop the coin on the enameled table.

The bird spurts away, but not far.
On a window ledge it waits, trying us
With one eye and then the other,
And when the boy whistles it comes to his hand.
From under his jacket he takes the small
Cage filigreed from pale, clean wood,
A Moorish bower where the bird enters,
A spoiled princess.

The priest and the students, bored now, turn away,
But the boy and I smile at each other,
Not decently nor gratefully, but with a certain love.
Each day now for a week I have bought
This same bird's life from this same boy
At this same table.
                      Why not?
The century being the century it is,
The role is a role worth perfecting.

Animal Crossing

My headlights drag a gray road
To me—a hundred feet a second, but
It seems always the same one hundred feet
Flowing beneath as a river whose source
We shall none of us find; whose deltas
We cannot imagine. The motion is not ours,
But a river's that pulls its shores
Along with it. Painted dividers spread their broken
Dashes like something that will never be spoken.
True, nothing is spoken, but
I see sliding into me a square of unlikely words.

Can it be true that animals cross here from woods
To woods in some old way? No, not true. Should
They set paw upon this moving road
Then they would flow with its aluminum flood,
Drift with silent fur and burning eyes
Upon a gray river—into me, under me.

Then let me, animals, let me, who motionless
Lie athwart the road, let me be the path you cross.
Let my stasis feel the raccoon's skeptical claws
Move across me toward lost groves.
Let the sharp-footed deer pierce my stayed flesh.
Let the little three-toed horse discover
Footing between my ribs, and so cross over.

A March on Washington
(For the Union and Confederate Dead)

Those black planes, whose speed makes silent air
Clap hands, seem to move now in the vast canary
Of the winter sunset as slowly as the stars
And flocks of birds that are also moving there
Dumbly, their definition lost in a yellow light
That is, like madness, too definite.

I pull my eyes from the window
And back to the striated, guitar-string icons
Of television where in the city of Washington
That poet—who wherever he turns smells brimstone—
Stands before his army of the helpless young.
They smile as he speaks, but he is not
Really speaking to them. His words go out
To the lady of history, that whore who muses
With Rubicon lips on her silken bed, who chooses
Only to hear what was never said,
Though she smiles to encourage the poet's words:
"You are so beautiful, lady, why can't you also be good?"

Be good, be good. She has not heard.
But I think someone has. Some small boy
Hears and gently gives up his toys.
From this moment on he will not bother
With thoughts of crawling back into mother
Or diddling sister or poisoning father
Or any of the fantasies usual and small
Which in the long run make people slightly bearable.
His followers, even now bored with mechano sets,
Are calmly waiting for him to say, "What
We must do to our brothers is wrong except it is good."

The poet's face suddenly races up the screen,
Disappears and reappears at the bottom line,

Jerks like an acrobat up the guitar strings.
The static shadow sprints backward in the seething stream.

I glance again at the window. The planes seem
Scarcely to have moved. Like snails
They leave on the sky a pearly trail.

Waiting in the Bone
(The Phi Beta Kappa Poem at the University of Michigan, 1972)

The red bird hung
Like a blood orange
Unmoving and round
In the gallow bones
Of the winter tree.

We wished to weep and could not.

Winter made us narrow. We went down
To live in underground
Chapels of bone.

We wished to weep.

Winter made us opaque.
By day we stared through black ice
Hanging like roots from eaves
And grooved by the Worm Sunlight.

We could not weep.

Winter wizened us.
At night we glared at the kinked wires
Of trees all sheathed
And tinkling with ice.
That ice drew down stars
Into the branches
Until the trees were full
Of stars, huge, quaking,
And repulsive. Withdrawing
Into bone drew the universe too close.
Eyelashes scratched
The glaze of a feral sky.

There was no distance, for we filled it.
There was no moment, for we could not move.

And we could not weep.

We were history and had no history.
We came, therefore, to admire crime
That owns the running criminal.
We came to admire the brute language
That does not own the brute.
We came to own a music
That did not admire us.

And so we burned our cities.
And so we killed our fathers.

In the bone Thebes from Troy
Is less than a step away.
There in the bone
Only blood is born.
Blood is mindless
But feeds the mind.
Blood is cruel.
But begets the soul.
In the shape of blood
The shape of tears is held.

Now that we have gone down
To where the blood is born,
Cities and fathers,
We shall come up from the bone.
We shall learn to weep again.

From the dazed ash of the winter plain
The red bird rises in the flames of the falling sun.
And as it rises, the red sky, the very color of the bird,
Leaches the bird's color, and we see a transparent bird.
Or perhaps we see the gleam on the threshold of space

Where the beloved sandal has paused, passed.
Or the arias
Of pure distance. Or tears
Falling upward
On the sky.

The Castrato Singer

Out there, the wolves are yodeling
Across valleys. As wind flings
A few rags of their song back into their teeth,
They snap, arch themselves up from forefeet
And again disgorge a broken arc
Of adolescent song on which they rise to shout
Down the smiling juries of the sky
Before they fall and, turning back
Among trees, brush chevrons of snow from the bark.

And I am in here, abstract and circular,
Beneath the eggshell of a gilded dome
Where my voice turns like a star.
Moving but never rising or falling, it comes
Orotund from the rosy O of my throat.
I sing to angels afloat in that moat
Of love from which they may not rise,
Though fall they can. They are messengers
Who do not understand the news
They bear. Nor do they listen to my voice.
The wolves who can no farther fall, though rise
They can—they listen. They listen, waiting like an opaque
Fear in the memory for my voice to break.

In the Gallery

The ninth century Attic vase,
Sparrow-tracked with the repeated lace
Of geometric beginnings smiles at the Warhol face
Repeated until it is meaningless
In the painting on the opposite wall.
We walk between them and say: "This is all.
We have endured much history, but this is all.
History has come back on itself. There is no more
To endure." And then the small lovers enter,
Bow to an audience of paintings which lean for-
Ward slightly toward them from the wall.

In the tundra's pale, natural
Light it may be the lovers would fail.
Sallow they might be
Among musk oxen knee-
Deep in the flowers of Labrador Tea.
But here in this yellow light electrical—
Which is theirs, where all
Their life has been delivered—they glow,
Their skins' faint city grime a patina
Of their richness. The phosphors
Of their hair greenly store
The tungsten light.
                       They flicker like foxfire
Across the room. Then, to our horror, disappear.
Surely now alarms will wail.
Surely the lovers were thieves. For the light fails.
The frames stand empty along the wall.
The vase sinks back into the potter's wheel.

Ramifications

Flying very high over Wyoming I see
A plateau I once had crossed
By horse—and thought it then
The least human of lands:
For mere mounds of colorless leavings
Rose from a colorless plain,
All of it looking like dust, but all of it
As hard as tufa. A land set as a rictus
To warn an invading sky
Whose light it would not take.

But here from the plane's window I see
It is the most human of lands.
Why, it is made like my hand.
From five mounds, thin
Cross-hatched washes run down
Until they intersect and make
Three riverbeds.
And it is like a leaf, as well.
It is like thought whose
Streams long to intersect
In a valley.

Yes, and I think if we had the eyes to see
The beginnings of all things,
What we'd see would be
Light flowing like rivers
Down mountains of light.

Old Leaves

It's not wind that takes old leaves
From trees in autumn. It's the next
Year's leaf buds. The buds dream them off.
But this last rainless summer perplexed
The buds, and so this tree
Has gone into winter with its old leaves.
A weird dust-green, they are almost no
Color at all. In wind they do not wave
But twitch on stiff stems. Light dazes
Them, and ice riddles. Without the bud's wild
Dream they can only hang on
As if they fought against some lively
Disease that troubles the dead.

God save, send the destroying child.

Frost Line

It's getting dark in this meadow.
I hardly see those flowers
Whose gray moon-mouths
Nuzzle my legs. But my skin tastes
Their coldness and guesses how their roots
Sink like long white hair
Down through moss to where
Snow-water wets the inch of soil
That millions of deaths
And millions of years
Have made. The hard frost
Is beneath that. I feel it
Under the moss that
So quivers and undulates
I have to balance
Myself by moving in a slow dance.
And I see now that all my life
I've been dancing on my grave.
There is nowhere else to dance.

The Sons of Medea

*Moth*er, was it only a minute past you called
Us back into the house? The day was going without
Sunset. It was as if sea and sky gave each other
To each other. We watched them grow together,
The sky rolling down as azure smoke
With a sound of waves to meet an azure
Mist rising with a sound of wind—
Until it was all one blue world through which
A comet fell, its blue wake staying then like a seam.
And you said, "That is how everything
Starts, a golden ball tossed. Up, down,
A celestial bribe. Then we act out the little
Plays that make gods certain of themselves.
If we did nothing for a day, they would die. We
Should find them hanging on their mountains like
The simulacra insects leave in certain seasons
On drying rocks. But we always act out
The play. And this one is almost done.
Come, little bluemilk ghosts, into the house."
You lit the lanterns at the threshold
And shut the door.   Since then for ages
You have been moving toward us. You move
Not as one walks through air, not as one
Swims through water, but as one would shoulder
A way through stone. Your face now leans
Vast and pitted on the sills of our eyes.
This close, you become one of those dolls we find
In the mounds of the old shore people.
We see you as circles, rounds of breast, belly,
Thigh. We are impaled, mother, on your roundness
And we cry out in the knowledge of
A certain ecstasy: that life has no violence,
No crime, no triumphant revenge. Only incest.

Now we know more, mother, than
Lullabyes and birds' eggs. But we are too little
To have a chorus sorting our fears
And making wisdom of our grief. Our fear, grief,
All these words we are speaking, writhe in one word,
The word we cry even as we move into it: "Mother!"

Men and Horses: Wyoming

You must think of some high meadow
Where the wind brings the taste of snow
Down from distant glaciers and dusts
The grass with harebells all the way to the rails
Of the corral where the man and the horse duel.

It is a matter of honor with them. Astray and idle
All summer, the horse has forgotten the saddle.
His long, blond mane is curdled with burrs.
Mounds of ticks glow ruby on his belly as he rears,
Boxing with forefeet at the man beneath
Him. But the man moves always just out of reach,
Always beyond the hooves and the teeth,
As he draws the noose tighter at the throat:—
Until they fall together, and the man sows
Grains of tobacco in the horse's eyes.
They lie then like dreams together, floating
On their hard breath, dust and dung-motes settling
Over them.

    Looking on from your distance, you will see
Only the old cruelty, the old hysteria
Of life. But for the man there, the vernal stir
Of the animal, its ragged smell of juniper
Touch all his body with such extravagance,
Such rasp and pang, that the dance
Of his nerves stops, and all his being slips
Into the darkness between things,
And for an instant he dreamlessly sleeps.
In this instant the horse, alert in pain, recalls the saddle,
The roots of the man growing deep. And how the bridle
And the taste of the bit pointed his hooves away from
Grassy fantasies toward something to be done.
He remembers how the feel of the man on his back once
Long ago brought forth from him the dense

Dream of horses from whose breasts the torsos
Of men spouted. Tutorial, these creatures spoke in verses
With the man's language that is more frivolous
Even than the language of birds, knowing a thousand ways
To say the three things that are worth the bother
Of saying. So dense the dream, that all others
Saw the creatures, too; saw them come down pale
From the foothills in moonlight in the shifty music of shale,
Moving the gay, pained heads forward upon the swell
Of tidal bodies.

                    The horse, awake with pain, says
To himself, "So dense this dream that even the man saw
Centaurs and thought they were his dream. What the man
Thought was wrong. I, the horse, dreamed it. Not the man."

The Water Hole

Lofty, the horse and I. Mountains are
No more than the low shore
Of this grassless plain
In whose center we've stopped. Sun
Is the burr in our hair as we look down
At water, this little blue sheet
Of water at the center, where a pink weed,
Like broken veins, grows flat on the white
Silt around. And so it is an eye
And the white of an eye. My clothes lie
Still bent in the grimace of toil
When I, naked, follow the tall
Unsaddled horse into water up to my thighs
And, sinking backward, open my eyes.
Between green nerve-strands of algae I gaze
At translucent bugs that like tailless kites
Jig toward the center of brown light.
An inch away, hair on the horse's leg grows out
Toward me like amber ferns.
The water he drinks rains back from his green
Mouth to mine. From his nostrils slime hangs down
To me. Through the living slime of this water
Eye we stare into the living slime of each other's
Eye until we trap God by not knowing whether
We see with the eye of horse or man or water.

Vermilion Cliffs

The sun, they say, is dying. True, the pulse
Of that life so pure that it kills
Has grown debonair. But the sun's beginning
Was only a beginning and its ending
Will be only an end. That is the way
Of suns—and ourselves. There is also a state
That is neither beginning nor end, and it
Is greater than we and greater than suns. Ponder
These red cliffs that hang, mile after mile, in Arizona—
I was going to say "that hang like a wave of blood
Frozen as a warning over the mammal's world." But that's
Not it. The cliffs are not blood. They are the harder stone,
The harder red, that stands when the soft is gone
Down trivial veins with the rain. Toward them,
Rather than the sun, it seems each cactus turns,
Discrete in its sleeve of light. And if we knew how stones
Turn, we should see that they, too, train
Themselves toward the cliffs. Shall we also turn
To find what is there whether sun shines
Or darkness shines, and with stones slowly feel
Ourselves become a body inhabiting a soul?

Falcons Hooded and Perched

You tell me, dear, of those smoky shapes
That come to the edge of our woods
And, quivering there like cobwebs,
Beckon you to come over to their side.

They are Cherokees, you think, long ago slain
In battle here, and now come to tell
You of a dim world that has no pain
Either of bone and flesh or heart and soul.

Dear, were there a place where we might lapse
All insubstantial and be of sorrow free,
There we'd think us ruled by weighty shapes
Favored by their mass to wreak their tyranny

On us. And we should sue, tempt all
Such gravity to rescue us from the idle swell
Of the wind-rivers of that heaven. But we'd not call
It heaven. We'd call it hell.

So stay and ask, what is love that bids you stay
And suffer. Oh, were it love of you alone
It could play magnanimous and say,
"Go, my dear dove, and moult your pain."

But my love for you is the love
Of God's love. God himself can little rest.
And the most of rest that we shall ever have
Will be as falcons hooded and perched on His flaming wrist.

Spring

Never does February end
But I know I shall find
You kneeling on frozen ground
And parting brown leaves until you find
On white leafless stems
A knot of violet buds,
Long-muzzled and turned down
Like the heads
Of lavender whippets.

                    I know,
Dear, nothing about the obdurate laws
That bring seasons in. But
When I think of spring I think of a law made
Uncertain and therefore free by brown hands
Searching blind in brown
Leaves for delicate, lavender heads.

II

Three Birds in Winter

The bird called cardinal
Strikes with his military beak at the window where
He sees himself a rival.
Grim he is and utterly sure.
I, too, have seen my enemy in a mirror,
But have turned away in despair.
I am no cardinal.

The bird called chickadee
Says from a leafless twig to me,
"Please, please, don't think I think you're an enemy."
His courage is to linger in his fear.
I, too, have seen vast alien shapes draw near,
But have fled. I am no chickadee.

The bird called owl
In the failing flow
Of the winter night coils
His claws about the frozen bough.
Terrible hunger sinks in his maw.
His blood falls in his flesh. Yet he calls,
Not to friend or foe
Or shape or face.
He calls with a lust more pure
Than chastity to the dreadful love that glows
In the vein of January.
I, too, I too. I may be an owl.

Music of Disaster

Above the telic sea-edge where we walk
The frigate birds are
Sealed in the parallels of a bar
Of music. Silent notes move north.
The sea glissandos silent to the south.
We stand; we stand and stare
Beyond the intact coda of birds,
Beyond the arpeggios of dolphins far
Out to sea. But it is our eyes, not theirs,
That declaim the spectral ocean
In cadenzas where we rise to tears, vision faltering
In the music, music faltering in the vision.

News from the Island Where
Executioners Are Exiled

for John Aldridge

We, who were the word breaking on every lip,
Spoke no word; we who were
The face dawning in every face
Covered our face with a hood. We
Who were you were, like history,
Exiled to this island. We the old hangmen,
Headsmen hidden like elder religions.

News comes in with the tide at dusk.
Shards, perforated by the minute problems
Of the sea, the glaze quite gone,
Stagger up like exhausted runners to gasp,
"Byzantium fell today. The gate was breached.
The burned shops lie open like ovens left to cool."

News. Once, the huge drowned hand
Of Poseidon drifted in, palm downward,
Half submerged and sluing like an overturned boat
In the writhing weed. In the morning sun
It dried and blew away like bits of parchment.

News. Today a lump of glass, rounded
And dulled by the sea floor, rolled to our feet,
An eyeball of the Sahara, opaque and blind,
Yet peering in the long unblinking arc of blindness.

And you who think you have exiled
The will and the act in an obscure
Museum, closed forever for repairs,
Remember that the broken city or the pious Christian murder;
Remember that the deathbed of the pharoahs, or the bouquet
Of anemones you picked this morning and carelessly
Dropped, having happened, happens forever.

The First Day out from Troy
(For Allen Tate's Seventy-Fifth Birthday)

On that afternoon when you saw
What was happening and knew
What was happening, like everyone
Else, you asked "What is happening?"
Then found yourself
A presence in the absence
Outside the gates of a burning city.

You thought then of a new city
Toward which you moved through a desert,
Your son's fist like a cocoon about
Your smallest finger, your father's arms
Like fallen rafters on your shoulders.
At first you conceived that city as the enduring
Disaster to be built upon the momentary disasters
Of oracles, foolishness of women, tournaments,
And wars among owls blinded by light.

By evening the murdering thirst by which
You were living drew you over azure sand
So fine your footfalls sent out ripples,
And, looking back at your father,
You saw how on his back his father clung
And on that one's back another father, fathers
Ascending to the beginning; on your back
The weight of them all. Meanwhile your son
Fluttered at your finger.

You knelt then in the windbreak where wind
Had shaped the sand like a long wave
About to break, and, digging an arm's length
Into the hollow below the crest, your hand at last
Found snow, perhaps the first snow of the world
Cached in the first sand. Snow melted in your hand.

Now you knew that the city would come to be.
Being great, it would surely be
That city at whose walls barbarians mass
To break the gates. As well as that city inhabited
By barbarians moaning for the gates to open and let them go.
Yet also that city of light, beheld not as light
Pressing upon the eye, but as light gathered by
The mendicant magnet of being leaning blind
From the eye as from a window.
Knowing that much, you finally knew
The founding of the city had already taken place—
There, in the rich freight on your back, and
There, in the beautiful childlike poverty
Of water running between your fingers.

The Cave of Hermes
(A tribute to Robert Penn Warren, 1977)

A thousand pardons, sir. I keep coming
Back to ask that you say once more
What you have said again and again
At the entrance to your cave.
There you stand, lean gentleman,
Exact on the pediment of your shadow.
"Come, friend," you say, "let us talk awhile
In the shade of the sun—the sun, you know,
Is the bearable shadow of unbearable light.
We ought not to ask more of art,
And so, of course, we do.
Very well, then. But let me admonish you:
I shall rob you of what little
You have. You will forgive me that.
At the same time I shall give
You what little I have.
You will *not* forgive me for that. Well,
I see already you are beginning to chill
In the brilliant umbrage of the sun.
Pray, step into the grotto. I apologize
For its simplicity. It owns no shrine,
No entablature, is nothing more
At all than polished stone.
I stabled the sun's mossy-faced cattle here once.
As they moved, their soft hair
Ground, palliated, glazed the rock. It shines.

"Remember—surely you don't think I'm robbing
You now?—remember your own shade within,
That is as nameless
And vague as a beast in a cave.
Let it move. Let it move
Great and powerless
Polishing the walls as it goes."

Winchester

Reading the engravature
On the Cathedral floor
About Jane Austen I become one
Of her loving survivors who are:
"Consoled by a firm though humble hope
That her charity, devotion, faith and purity
Have rendered her soul acceptable
In the sight of her redeemer."
That is exactly where her busy knitting needles meant
To get. That is exactly the sentiment
To end the sundries of drawing rooms and tea,
Which comprise the bliss of her originality.

But in this city of Winchester, just beyond
The tea cup, just around
The corner, it is apt to be rather late
In September and apt to be raining.
The cold damp flattens the senile nap of your coat.
You press against walls that are softly falling
On you like a collapsed lung.
At which moment you hold in your autumn arms
A fossil of summer, whose heart is so slowed
That you listen to its music as a child
Suspended in mystic luxury listens to
A music box, nearly run down,
Waiting in the lengthening interval
For one more teased and plectral note.

Jane Austen, John Keats, how much you need
Each other. How much I need you both.

Lines for the English

Dusk descends, as I suppose
It always has
On the River Tavey that because
Of peat beds runs red,
Yet never makes you think of blood
Or fire.

      In an hour empires fall,
But in a century nothing at all
Of importance happens. What is important is
To know that courtesy is stronger
Than ideas; and morality is never a consolation prize
You get when you give up power.
To know that is to know
Don Juan or Auden always
Returns in the last canto
To the banks of the red Tavey or the mental
Thames, as dusk descends and a thousand gentle
Clerks, snubnosed like so many William Blakes, ascend
The sky of a land more green
And pleasant than any New Jerusalem.

Some Marvelous Quarry

He, walking home from school,
Saw something that looked like a hole
In the February swamp's blurred shoals
Of thawing ice and freezing pools.
And because he had to see what it was
He leapt and slid and fell on bars
Of ice until at last he lay out flat,
His face only a foot
From the mound of a porcupine caught
In the arms of a going and coming winter.
No quill stirred in the wind. The unwary
Eyes gleamed as though fixed on some marvelous quarry.
Had there been stench, he'd have known
It as the stench of death. Had there been
Maggots pumping in their cylinders
Of greed he'd have known it as
The death he knew. But this was changeless,
Perfected, the unmoving shadow of everything
That moves.

    At home, of course, he had
To be punished for clothes muddy and wet,
For books spoiled. But since he was one who easily wept,
Even for soft rebukes, his father only played,
Half-smiling, at bringing down the limp belt
On his outstretched hands.
The boy paled but could make no tears.
They looked then, father and son,
At each other with separate fears.
They guessed much, but neither could bear
To believe no punishment would make the boy
Flinch and cry and forget what he now knew.

First Day of School

It is my first day in school,
And what I have learned is
I must roll up my sleeves and make
Something from clay served like a slab
Of gray ice cream on my desk.
But to roll up my sleeves!
For now everyone can see how skinny my arms
Are. The gray clay dries
On them, the childish hairs standing stiff,
And I have at the end of the day
Made nothing from clay
But shameful little ordures
Mottled with fingerprints.

It is my first day in school,
And what I have learned is
My pants, once my brother's and cut down
To fit, show all the stretch
Wrinkles of his husky thighs as they hang
Like fluted drapery on my skin and bones.
And everyone knows, knows this
And knows I am not right,
And my religion is crazy,
And my family is not rich.

It is my first day of school,
A day in which days and days pass,
Until a bell rings, and I rise,
Wetting my pants, and it feels
Like a bell ringing down my legs,
And I run to the doors
And fall down all the stairs. On the final
Stair I sit in the falling afternoon,
Wet, my knee bleeding
And listen to a gray crone saying

Over and over again, her face
Cracking like ice in all directions
As she speaks, "You will
Never have any success."
And when I say, "But I didn't cry
When I cut my knee," she says
"You will never be brave enough
To cry. You will always just sit
Staring at the sun till it looks like a moon,
With your mouth turned down. No one
Will ever choose you for a side in a game.
No one will ever vote for you
For anything, anything at all."
The words give me a bitter calm,
And when I look at the crone more closely
I see it is my sister, bloodying her handkerchief
On my knee, saying they were worried when
I was late, and she had come
To find me and bring me home.

Oh home!

Achilles and the Tortoise

Monsters wash ashore,
The smell of hydraulic densities
Issuing from the fissures of improbable
Bodies that broke as they fell
Toward us from the inverted Everests
Of the sea.

Furred prodigies
Come to the edge of the clearing
And stare at us to see what they
Will become.
Phosphorescent ships hover at twilight
Above the garden. Through translucent bows
We see the long, dispassionate face we shall achieve.

The feral footprint is there in the woods;
The garden is blackened by astral flame.
The eyes of monsters on the beach
And our eyes move together
Like sea pools settling their differences.

Imprinted by the spoor of *was* and *will*,
We frolic in the gap
Where we overtake something that
Waits for us by running away.

Heliogabalus

He danced for the people the dance
He'd learned as a priest of the Asiatic sun.
As blind as a flower in the sun
He moved in the memorized paths
Of the blind. And when at the end of the dance
In a play of castration his knife cut
The burning bladder of bull's blood
Tied at his groin, and he smiled,
They, the Romans, were not shocked. They
Were only puzzled as they turned away,
Unable to say if it was small or great,
This weight they felt lifting from them.

What of it, if at the end, he tried to hide
From assassins and did not stare
At death man to man like a Caesar?
The people were tired of bad epics,
Wanted nothing more than a good cry.

Chasms

I wonder why we come again and again
To these places where footpaths suddenly end,
And beneath us lies a chasm. Someimes it is
A sea like a vast grapevine
We watch, its veined, overlapping leaves
Shifting out of phase until they break at the horizon.
Sometimes we come to these great holes
In the desert where nothing shifts at all,
And, it seems, will never shift again and yet
Remains all unfinished. See, how from the red
Bed of an exinct river rise
These eery half-formed images.
Here is almost an arch, but the ochre stone forgot
To finish its guess. Here is half a catapult.
Yet how lovely unfinished ideas are.
How delicate the partial caltrop, the lacy conjecture
Of golden mantelets, ruby cities that as far as we can see
Glow in the bloodless blood red abyss.

Which, we ask, should we feel the more:
The vastness or the delicate fantasies?
In the end we feel neither. And this is the chasm's use.
We can only turn away. We turn, plotting to design
True arches, polities more perfect than
The overlapped leaves of a vine.

III

The Garden of Medusa
for Caroline Gordon

You have the choice whether to go or not.

You will be seated at a table, perhaps,
On a headland. Other diners have gone.
The waiter has cleared his face like an abacus
And departed. The playful yachts
Have fled, and far beneath you the last
Child has left the beach where the sand
Is turning blue, and the fingering
Of land by sea ceases between
The ebb and the rising. You may ebb then;
Or rise, stand among cobalt bee orchises,
Then walk through the furze on the cliff edge,
Feeling birds start from their nests at
Your ankles. Your next step will have wind
For an instant under the descending toe
And rising heel, and you will come down,
When you come down, in her garden.

You will hear the dead-leaf rustle of serpents
And catch the odor of clay and cold violets.
You have another choice then. You may
Observe her in the dark mirror you will find
Has grown in the palm of your hand.
You can see there how the serpents churn,
Unravelling the cloth of the world.
Below them you will see eyes colder
Than tourmaline cast down toward lips
That have drawn all body's blood
Into themselves and, swollen, sweat blood
Through transparent skin.
If you carry this face in your mirror
Out of the garden you will defeat
Your enemies (though there will be no end of them).

And pass under the pale poplar and through
The gate still open just enough for you
To pass, who have just enough strength to pull it to.

The Garden of Eros

All night you will crawl in the caul of sleep,
Wondering where the garden is and how
You may enter. All day your eyes
Will grind the angle of the lids,
Seeking in the pit outside
The gate of sight for that garden.
You will not see it in the closeness
Of dreaming; nor yet in the distance of waking.
Nor will you enter the garden.
The garden will enter you.

Having entered you—this garden—you
Are its keeper. You wander among
The discord of specimens,
You speak to it in innuendoes,
Cajoling inharmonious deathbeds
With grievous puns. Terrible fricatives,
Sibilants, and plosives of joking despair
Come from your mouth to force
The garden into order, but the garden
Only walks out of you, and you find
You are singing the song you supposed
Would be sung to you between the moist
Hedges of a perfect maze. You sing
To yourself in a retreating garden: "Oh come,
Be lucky and in me drown.
Be lucky, be daring, come in,
Come down, come drown
In the endless deep of the deep deep skin."

The Garden of Aphrodite

Remember, you never go to this garden,
You only return. Returning,
You find it altered, but not
In the way other things alter.

Let us say it is spring when you come
To the rondure of her keep. The doves
Will rise at your approach, but you
Will hear the creak of their wings
Before you see the wings. And the grass
On which she stands will be the color
Of tomorrow's grass. As always, she will say,
"I don't believe I have really seen *you* before."

You have sternly intended to say,
"You never remember me though my past
Is mortgaged to your future. Your
Children are monsters, cunning androgynes,
Sly hermaphrodites. I doubt they can be mine."

But before you can say what you were
Going to say she will have said, "All
The monsters of the world are yours."
And you say instead, "Your arms smell
As flowers smell before they smell like flowers."

The Garden of Ariadne

If you come to this garden at noon
You see only that myrtle conceals
The stones of the wall; the priapus at the gate
Has lost aspect and seems no more
Than a milestone; while the old fig
Holds few leaves and no fruit
In the astonished O of its serpentine limbs.
But at night, in the prospects of moonlight,
Tree, wall, statue densify like the past in
The silvery spume of the present. The woman
Of the garden holds something you almost recognize
In one hand, and her eyes turn to water as
She slowly turns to face you. "I have seen
You before," she says, "though I cannot remember where—
Damascus, was it, Thera, Los Angeles?
You were one who as evening came on always
Found your school books unbearable and slipped
Into the streets to walk half the night
With a friend, talking of the components
Of your love; murmuring of the arctic spectrum
Of friendship, until within your ghastly virginity
A glacial Eros and wisdom-burning-in-rut
Fell like light into the same space.
Then you went home, your knees giddy on
The stairs, and your parents, who would have been
Slightly amused had you reeked of wine,
Sat up in their bed and cried, 'What is that flame
Festering in the boy's hair? What is it?
What is wrong?'

"And now, because at times you turn in at the brothel,
Because your friends bore you and you have nothing
To say, and because you do not believe in truth,
You come to the garden of one who betrayed
Brother and father and was betrayed

By a love, hoping I can flay the thickness
Of your life until your light shines through again.

"I must tell you—that friend of your youth,
When you left him in the streets, went
Always to the wineshops and the arms
Of some bestial lover whom he wittily told
Of your madness. Yet today he is the hierophant
Of a celibate cult and writes hymns
To a phosphorescent god he never names.

"You are welcome here, as is everyone,
And everyone sooner or later comes.
But you must see that this is a garden
You do not enter until you realize
You have never left it. You have lived your life
Here, as you should, in preparation, as
Your holy friend would say, for the time when,
Cracking like a carnival egg, you will spill
The motes of yourself back into that whirling flotation
Where it is well to be used to reversals, drastic surprise."

The Garden of Maia

Suppose, in a high ravine you feel
The mind of rain hypnotic in the hush.
And you may then see how milky green light,
Shuddering up from a swollen creek, meets
The slow drip of light from a tree's halo.
And there, there before you at this meeting,
Light is substance, as stone falls through stone,
And rain colder than rain begins in your hair.

When you are cold and wet enough that
The weight of clothes proves nakedness
You will find beyond a threshold of violets
The grotto you scarcely wanted to find.
Press your face into that shade as hard as stone.
Press until your pupils widen to meet gloom with gloom.
At first you will see nothing but the webbing
Of bats on the walls, how they cling
To each other, soft and starving, but safe
In the colonal sleep of their warm
Abjection. Beyond them you will finally see
Her ancient eyes shrewd and burning.

Is that shadow a robe of fur she wears,
You will ask, or the fur of her body?
And asking, you will feel a lust that will almost
Kill you, but as you move to enter the cave
Her voice bars you with the sound of
The laughter of sons castrating their father
And the groan of fathers devouring their sons.

"You cannot enter," she says. "It has been
Too long. I am nothing now, though I am back
Of everything. I am not here, though I
Am behind what is here. Go now and forget
Me. Or, if you think of me at all, think

Of me as the white violet crushed beneath
Your instep. Its will gathers to lift you."

The Garden of the World

Here, at this point where the gate dissolves,
And you are neither within nor without;
Here, where no lady, ironical or grave,
Tends the revenant dead-nettle;
Here, where the botanist has named and collected
And the pressed specimen shifts on its silhouette,
Here is where you are.

                    The dry wind
That finds you has not been seeking you.
The yellowed alder leaf that curls back on itself
And falls, scribbling in your hair, brings
No message. Gray roots in hard land do not have
Your benefit in mind as they press the intaglio of
A pebble into themselves. The fleshy undulance of
The opaki rocks upon the bushland for the sake
Of fleshy undulance. The pallid termite
Meets you as a brother in the darkened
Laboratory where you both make do,
And having nothing to praise, praise the act of praise.
Here, at this point where the gate dissolves.

The Garden of Niobe

At that moment when by accident
Your music becomes so strange and virtuous
It alters the ear, and your rival retreats
Into the down of his body,
You become the undivided creature
Of your smile, a smile with no haze of doubt.
That smile will be cruel.

You will need nothing then; nevertheless, you
Will find yourself seeking a certain garden
As if it were a need.

                It will be an
Early summer evening when you leave your beached
Boat and walk toward the cleft in a headland.
Before you enter the cleft, look up
To where snow, caught in a hollow rift
Below the summit, is touched by the long
Rays rising from a sun awash in the sea.
Where the rays touch, water darkens the stone
And ferns hang like wet lashes.
Walk, then, into the cleft.
As dusk thickens you will hear
A music strange even to your ears.
As this music, older than birdsongs,
Circles down on you, you will see
Flickers of flame descending the cliffs,
Converging, parting until you see the flames
Are children gliding along the space of a game.
In the vise between their eyelids and
Their brows they hold fireflies.
They run, trilling, toward you in a line,
Separate and are gone. But if you are lucky one
Will return, take the fireflies from an eye and put
Them in your hand. They will give enough light

For you to walk back in the night.
If you have been this lucky, perhaps
You will be even luckier and know
That all music is a lost self,
And the lost self returns to you only when
Your grief for him makes you kind.

At your boat your smile will shift like a tear,
As you lean down to kiss the rival
Who is praising your music.

The Garden of Prometheus

If you travel over high mountains in June
It may well be that, looking down into a glacial cut,
You will see how the ice-giant desperately thrusts
His arms into gullies to hold to hills,
His gray nails scrabbling in the grit, as he falls,
Slowly pulling the world with his somber declension.
Above his strained body drift great birds,
Shimmering riffles in the dark sky-stream,
Uttering those cries that will never be words,
But are the ecstasy pure beyond cause
And are pure lamentation without object.
They skim, wheel beyond him, yet
Return to log the unmaking by day,
The making by night, the check
And glide of the giant's fall as they,
Returning, fall with him, raptors rapt
In the dream's lethargic punctuality.
And you, flowing in the flow you watch,
Will see how the water of agonies wets
A little soil toward which the dream
Progresses. In that small field anemones
Blaze briefly; fennel floats its frost-green flame.

There is the garden from which you cannot fall.